M. Lawrence .

MIME AND IN

MIME AND IMPROVISATION

Alison Muir and Patricia Hammond

OBERON BOOKS
LONDON

First published by Oberon Books Ltd (incorporating Absolute Classics),
521 Caledonian Road, London N7 9RH, in association with the
London Academy of Music and Dramatic Art, Tower House, 226
Cromwell Road, London SW5 OSR

ISBN 1 84002 012 1

Cover design: Andrzej Klimowski

Typography: Richard Doust

CONTENTS

Alison Muir

MIME

Acknowledgements

Photographs: Many thanks to Pat Knight, the Bushey School of Dance and Drama and Harrison College students.

With special thanks to Fiona, Jim, Keith and Mary for all their support.

INTRODUCTION

The use of gesture is a universal communication and one which harks back to the beginning of civilisation.

Mime, which uses the medium of body movement and facial expression, has its origins in the early forms of Greek and Roman drama but achieved widespread popularity in sixteenth century Italy. During this time, troupes of performers provided improvised drama known as Commedia dell' Arte using established characters, each with their own recognised posture and movement patterns to complement the facial masks which most of the company wore.

The Commedia spread to France with the influence of playwrights such as Molière and did much to inspire the artistry of mime. This continued until the mid-nineteenth century, and Jean-Baptiste-Gaspard Deburau, famous for his performance of Pierrot, was the last of the great mimes of that era.

Today, the name Marcel Marceau is synonymous with mime for many of us, and rightly so, since his work achieved the re-establishment of mime as an independent art form. One measure of this is the International Mime Festival which gathers in London every January, bringing together an exciting range of artists from all over the world.

The LAMDA Mime syllabus offers a carefully graded approach to the progression of artistic ability and technique through the attainment of specific skills at each level.

I have taken the components of grades I – IV as my focus for this handbook. Activities can be tailored to the needs of the student depending on whether individual or group work is required. Mime is also an excellent way to assist performance in acting and improvisation since increased awareness and use of non-verbal attributes such as posture, gesture, facial expression and proximity, enhance the integrity of characterisation.

A word about the presentation of mime: do choose clothes which allow freedom of movement such as leggings, track bottoms, jazz shoes. Flexibility is all important to the credibility of any mime; begin at an advantage!

Enjoy and learn from the activities. Have fun!

EATING AND DRINKING

Waking up the face first is important as it makes the face come alive and directs the focus of energy to where it is needed.

This section concentrates mainly on the senses involved in eating and drinking. The use of the mouth is important in demonstrating the contrasts which need to be shown in terms of texture, temperature and so on. Activities are involved for theme purposes, enabling the student to create mimes in different contexts as opposed to building a scene.

VISUAL AIDS AND OTHER STIMULI

- photographs of foods are good as a stimulus
- 'smell' games invoking different foods
- the real thing! Particularly good before the taste game: try sugar, salt, lemon juice or sherbet to wake up the taste buds

FACE ENERGY: THE WARM UP

1. tap your face all over with your fingertips, forehead, cheeks, nose, mouth, chin
2. screw up the face tightly and relax it
3. open the face wide in surprise, don't forget the mouth!
4. open the mouth wide and yawn, ahhh – that's better!
5. chew an everlasting toffee – will it never end?

The Taste Game

Have four imaginary cups in front of you:

- one contains something nice
- one contains something which is not nice

- one contains something – you're not sure how it tastes at first, mmm, that's nice!
- one contains something – you're not sure, once again then – YUK!

Play the game in pairs, choosing one of the four items at random.

Can the person watching tell which one you are drinking?

Smells Great – Or Not So Great

Imagine a delicious smell connected with food or drink. For example:

- hot chocolate
- newly baked bread
- roast dinner
- donuts

Now imagine something not so delicious. For example:

- burnt toast
- raw fish
- boiled sprouts
- boiled meat

Try and 'smell' each one in turn. Note how reactions are different each time. For example, one might be an overpowering smell that hits you immediately. Another, one that grows on you.

Tasty Textures

Food and drinks have different textures and compositions, so we eat them in different ways. If you have photographs of items, try grouping them into different categories before practising:

Hard:	carrot	apple
Chewy:	toffee	gum
Soft:	yoghurt	custard

| **Slippery**: | blancmange | banana |
| **Fizzy**: | lemonade | sherbet |

Temperature Teasers

Experiment with miming the following:

| **Hot**: | soup | curry |
| **Cold**: | ice cream | iced tea |

Taster Placers

What food and drinks would you expect to find:

- in a lunch box
- on a best china plate
- in a takeaway carton
- in a flask
- in a china cup and saucer
- a sports drink container

Try eating and drinking your chosen items from these.

Personality Posers

Try eating and drinking a selection of foods in different ways:

- greedily
- slowly
- fastidiously
- thoughtfully
- quickly
- sloppily

Food and Drink Themes

In pairs or groups, practise the following:

Preparing a meal:

- in a top class hotel
- a fast food chain

- Sunday lunch at home
- getting ready for a picnic
- a wedding feast
- pancake day

Eating Out:

American diner: milkshake and hamburger
seaside: fish and chips
chinese restaurant: fortune cookies
at Hallowe'en: dunking apples
at a fairground: candy floss
school canteen: lunch
cocktail party: wine and nibbles

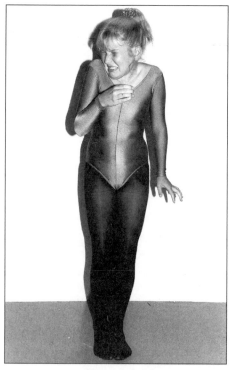

Horrid drink

LOCATION

First of all, you need to give some thought to your chosen location in order that your audience can visualise it. Consider the following:

Is the physical environment:

- rural and rocky
- ugly and urban
- cluttered and claustrophobic
- a tropical paradise

Is the temperature:

- scorching and sizzling
- raw and icy cold
- controlled by air conditioning
- stuffy and humid
- wet and damp

What people might you find there:

- crowds
- couples
- children
- a cosmopolitan mixture

What noises might you hear:

- people talking/laughing/shouting
- birds and animals
- machines
- natural elements eg: sea, river, rain
- music

What can you smell:

- a burning fire
- a sharp burst of the ozone
- petrol fumes
- lovely fresh air

PLACES TO BE

Playground	Seaside	Bowling Alley
Cinema	Restaurant	Fairground
Club	Festival	Concert Hall
Rock Climbing	Pot Holing	Park

It is a good idea to start work in familiar surroundings, and then extend to other places. Try to avoid the stereotypical scenarios and have fun exploring all the possibilities that offer themselves to you.

At the same time, remember that what you present must have clarity and so avoid obscure interpretations where the meaning is not apparent.

WORKING WITH
THE HANDS AND FEET

Hands and feet are obviously at the extremities of body movement and the focus on them is a good introduction to the greater awareness and control needed for the body in mime.

Apart from the benefits gained from the isolation of these two areas, it is an important teaching point. Students new to mime can feel less inhibited about moving certain areas as opposed to the body as a whole.

Again, warm ups are important preparation for each area of activity. They help to free up unconscious tension, and pinpoint awareness to the specific part of the body to be used in mime.

HANDS

THE WARM UP:

- shake loose as if drying your hands in the air
- extend sharply, like a witch or wizard casting a spell, or the film character Edward Scissorhands in a bad mood
- play the piano, each note at a time
- scoop up sand (fingers together, elbows still)

Wrists:

Hold both hands up at 90 degrees to the arm. Drop one then bring back. Do the same with the other hand and repeat the whole exercise several times.

ACTIVITIES

The size and weight, texture and temperature of what you are handling is naturally very important to the accuracy of presentation.

Touch

Get used to the shape and texture of the following groups of items by feeling each one in turn:

Soft	**Prickly**
Swan's down	Cactus
Velvet	Rose stem

Slippery	**Rough**
Polished table	Snake skin
Marbles on a tray	Emery board

Squidgy	**Hot**
Playdough	Jacket potatoes
Clay	Hot chestnuts

Size

Convey the size of objects through the dexterous use of fingers and thumb. Show the difference in size between:

a glass bead	a *lego* brick
a football	a real brick

Weight

You need to study how the body is used in resistance to a weighty object. Try lifting a heavy suitcase as an experiment. See how you lean *away* from the weight to balance yourself rather than *towards* it.

PUTTING IT ALL TOGETHER – THE HANDS HAVE IT!

- carry hot plates
- hold a big wet fish
- eat hot chips
- pick up a big hairy spider

- aim a ball into a basketball net
- pick a coin out of green slime
- slice a lemon with a sharp knife
- pick up broken glass
- switch channels on the TV with the remote control
- light a candle
- try on a ring
- make a magic ball disappear then reappear
- mould a clay pot
- free a butterfly through an open window

Picking up a big hairy spider

FEET

THE WARM UP:

- stretch the foot along the floor and point – four times
- stretch the foot along the floor then press the ball of the foot into the floor – four times

- extend the foot up and point on the floor – four times
- balance the foot in the air and rotate – four times
- repeat the warm up with the other foot

Walking Patterns

Walk:

- normally
- in a hurry
- slowly and thoughtfully

These activities help raise the awareness of the body in space and, in particular, the patterns brought about by our feet. Try also:

rhythm of life: clap a rhythm and walk to it

the accent engenders: read out a passage of dialect and let the rhythm of the accent lead the way

numbers game: think of a sequence eg: 412 763 and then trace out a ground pattern of these numbers by walking through the sequence in small steps

hopscotch: a popular children's game, good for the balance and co-ordination of the feet

Different Shoes

Try walking as if you were wearing the following:

High Heels	Shoes that are too tight
Ballet Shoes	Leaky shoes
Doc Martens	Wellington boots full of jelly
Barefoot	

Surfaces

Think of how you might walk across the following surfaces, imagining that you are in appropriate footwear. This means that you have to think of what you are wearing as well as where you are:

- thin ice
- a booby-trapped floor
- a muddy field
- a cave covered in snakes
- a swamp full of crocodiles
- a ball park
- in cold water
- a floor covered in balloons

Footsteps – a class activity:

Divide the class into two groups, group A turned facing away from group B.

Group B take it in turns to create a sequence of footsteps.

Group A listen and ask themselves:

- how are they walking – quickly? In a measured way?
- what kind of tread – light and gentle? Heavy and paced?
- where could they be going?
- who could they be?

MOVEMENT AND CHARACTER

Work on movement is involved here as a precursor to character mime. A convincing characterisation is one in which the movement and gesture of the role are a reflection of the thoughts which precede behaviour. In order to reach that point, we need first to establish a greater awareness of the body itself.

The balance of our bodies is sustained by postural reflexes which operate below the level of consciousness. This occurs naturally in animals and young children but less so as we grow, where the stresses and strains of modern life cause alterations to the body state. These interfere with natural balance and prevent it from being employed effectively. In addition, postures such as a prominent head thrust or hunched shoulders may become a habitual part of our daily stance and movement. Techniques such as the Alexander Technique can help us become aware of such unnecessary tensions and bring posture back to its more natural state.

MOVEMENT FOR CHILDREN

Visual and auditory images are very useful in promoting the different states of body tension.

Sounds Around

Collect music of contrasting tempo and mood.

Begin walking normally around the room. Be aware of how the hands and arms swing loosely as you walk.

Listen to two very different pieces of music. Think of how they differ and words that describe their mood eg. fast, slow, tense, dark, happy, light.

Move to each piece of music in turn, using the whole body to express the words that have been found to describe it.

Examples might be:

- Night on a Bare Mountain – Rimsky Korsakov
- The Firebird – Stravinsky
- Entry of the Gladiators – Fucik
- Airlane – Gary Numan
- Oxygene – Jean Michel Jarre
- Speed of Life – David Bowie
- Morning Glory – Jamiroquai

Toy Procession

Walk stiffly as a soldier then move as a floppy doll.

Come to life as a puppet and finish by collapsing back into a heap as the strings are released.

Waxwork Figures

Adopt a pose as a favourite waxwork, then slowly melt.

OLDER STUDENTS

The following is a $3\frac{1}{2}$ minute work out designed to warm the muscles and isolate each part of the body for muscular awareness and agility. It works well to a soft reggae rhythm, but any four time music would do.

1. Shake out the body, working from:
   Hand – arm – shoulder – whole arm
   Repeat with the opposite arm
   Foot – leg – hip – whole leg
   Repeat as before

2. Take three steps to the right, click fingers. Repeat left. Do this twice.

3. Three steps to the right, shoulder high clap. Repeat left. Do this twice.

4. Three steps to the right, higher than shoulder clap. Repeat left. Repeat sequence again.

5. **Shoulders** – slowly rotate right shoulder four times. Rotate left shoulder four times. Rotate both shoulders together, four times.

6. **Head** – centre head and look straight forward. Using clean, sharp but not jerky movements – drop head forward then back four times. Repeat turning side to side four times, then tilt side to side four times. Come back to centre position between each movement.

    Make sure that the head is dropped carefully to the correct position, not thrown into it.

7. **Hips** – Keep the knees soft by bending them a little – start this section by keeping the body in centre position, ie shoulders over hips over knees over toes.

    Isolate hip movement alternating right and left four times, coming back to the central position between each isolation.

    Combined movements – slide from right to left four times.

    Repeat the isolation, tilting the hips forward and back four times (again working from the central position) then four combined movements.

8. **Ribs** – Hold arms out to the sides in central position.

    Push the ribs to the right – bring back to central position, then to the left and repeat – four times.

    Keep the rest of the body still.

    Combine the movements and slide from right to left four times.

9. **Lunges** – Place feet wide apart and bend the right knee, turning the rest of the body towards it.

   Bend the right knee slowly keeping the left leg straight. Push forward gently and release four times and then repeat left. Keeping the legs wide apart, turn the feet out and face front, bend the knees.

   Slide the lunge from right to left – four times in all.

10. **Back Stretches** – Kneel on all fours, head in line with spine. Arch the back and drop the head. Stretch the back and raise the head.

    Four movements in each position.

11. **Stretches** – Sit on the floor and tuck the left leg behind you by bending the left knee.

    Place the right leg out at a diagonal in front. Bend the body over the right leg for four times and repeat with the left leg, tucking a bent right leg behind you. (See Fig 1)

Fig 1

Do not push the stretch any further than is comfortable.

Bring legs together, roll over onto the knees and stand up slowly. Finish the exercise by standing feet apart.

Bend the knees slightly and drop over so that the arms swing loose. (See Fig 2)

Fig 2

Pull up slowly – imagine that you are placing one vertebra at a time on top of the other. Make sure that head and shoulders come up last of all.

Repeat the exercise, ending on the balls of the feet and raising the arms in front.

Slowly lower the heels and arms; be aware of the symmetry and lightness of posture.

Body State

Lie down, tense up each part of the body in turn, then relax it – feet, legs, hips, stomach/chest, shoulders, arms, hands, head.

Tense the whole body and hold for a count of three, then relax.

Bring in mental relaxation to ensure a harmony between the mental and physical states. Lie with eyes closed and imagine you are:

- shipwrecked and exhausted on a beach
- moulded into a floor of super jelly which is supporting your weight
- floating in a large rubber ring

Or you could try:

- visualising a colour
- following a mental journey story
- turning your head to one side and visualise yourself in an activity in which you have taken part – the image is bright and clear. Repeat turning your head to the other side and visualise yourself in the same activity – but this time the image is blurred and faded – as if it was a sepia photograph of something which happened a long time ago

MENTAL WARM UP

These help to sharpen the mind and make responses alert, in readiness for movement work.

For younger children, try popular games such as Port Starboard or Simon Says.

For older students, the following game – which is a group one – helps to develop alert concentration as well as being a lot of fun:

Circle Crossing

The group form a circle with one person in the centre.

Two people within the circle agree to change places – this is done by nods, winks and eye contact – but no speech.

As they change places, the person in the centre has to try and reach one of the vacated places first – thus leaving one person in the middle.

It is best to start this game quite slowly because it speeds up of its own accord as the responses of the participants become quicker. Once this happens you can introduce greater complexity by having another pair agree to cross – so that there are four people crossing at once, with one person in the middle. Build from there if you wish, until the whole group is on the go, alert, and searching for the next opportunity to cross.

PRINCIPLES OF MOVEMENT

The work of *Laban is important here. He looked on movement as a two-way language process through which the body communicates by sending and receiving messages.

He stated that there are certain basic movement principles to which all living matter conforms, and that to select one's movement behaviour allows the exploration, and thus development, of character.

Concentrating on four basic movements:

Gliding   **Punching**

        Slashing   **Floating**

Apply these first to movement of the body in its own space. Feel the different moods and physical shapes engendered by each type.

---

*Rudolf von Laban (1879-1958). Often acknowledged as the father of modern dance theory, his *Laban Notation* is the best known of today's dance notation systems.

Next, involve the movement in an actual activity with the body, maintaining the characteristics of each movement type.

For example:

gliding: a parascending lesson

punching: a boxing match

slashing: cutting through undergrowth

floating: an astronaut in space

MOVEMENT ACTIVITIES

Practise the following to extend your use of movement.

Individual:

- dance in metal boots
- score a winning goal in the World Cup
- kick a ball to find out it is made of concrete
- walk along a busy street, keeping tabs on someone without being seen
- box the invisible man
- find your way through a maze
- cross a lake by means of stepping stones

Pairs or Groups:

- sculpt a pose – the 'sculptor' shapes the posture of the 'model' or 'models'
- walk along a tightrope
- wind up a mechanical toy
- carry a ladder
- play tug o'war
- have a game of tennis in slow motion
- row a boat

High Tension

Remember the states of tension needed in movement in order to show resistance. Practise:

- flying a kite
- climbing a tree
- rolling a snowball

Animal Crackers

Studying the movement of animals is a good precursor to character work. It allows the student to observe, and then recall with accuracy, what they have seen.

With younger students, encourage them to show the movement of the following animals and also the differences between them. Use photographs to provide a visual aid to your discussion on movement:

- rabbit – jumps on all fours
- kangaroo – jumps on hind legs
- monkey – has strong arm movements
- caterpillar – undulates as it moves
- snake – slithers along the ground

Be creative – make up your own animal and decide on a movement for it. In Eastern religion, there is an animal called the Makarat which was created by the Buddha to bring together the seven best features of different animals. Thus, it has the tail of a peacock (beauty), the body of a fish (suppleness), the feet of a lion (strength), the nose of an elephant (keen smell), the eyes of a monkey (good sight), the ears of a pig (acute hearing) and the mouth of a crocodile (strong teeth). Now – how would you move as a Makarat?

For older students, focus on the specific ways in which animals move. Try a study of a pet animal or take a trip to the zoo – and *observe*!

CHARACTER DEVELOPMENT

Entrance Mimes

These are a good way to move onto the development of character as they encourage the student to *be* the role from the moment the mime begins. Entrance mimes enhance the immediacy of the start and assist continuity with the moments which may have preceded it.

Try the following:

- a thief entering a house
- a restaurant owner going to speak to noisy guests

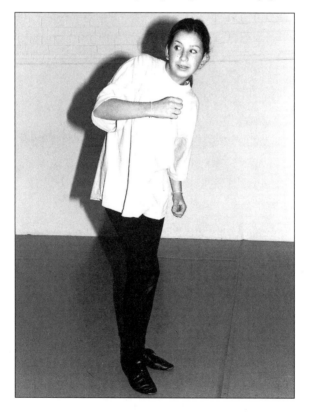

Entrance Mime – a teenager coming home late

- a teenager coming home late
- a pupil going to see the Head Teacher having been caught playing truant
- a contestant preparing for the screen to go back on *Blind Date*
- a contestant entering the dressing room having fought the *Gladiators*
- realising you have the winning lottery numbers and rushing in to find your ticket
- an actor coming on stage for an audition

Picture Poses

Think of a character. Start an activity and then freeze the moment. Concentrate on the character at the crystallisation of that moment:

- trying on tight shoes
- working on a shop till
- rolling out pastry
- getting lost in London
- walking home on a cold winter's night
- dodging a ticket inspector

Try the same idea in pairs or groups, with each person assuming a different role in the following:

- the wedding party
- stuck in a traffic jam
- the last day of school
- expedition to Snowdonia
- the card game
- the train station
- arrival at a holiday destination
- a game show

Picture Poses – the card game

Develop a situation in which one of the following may be found:

Window Cleaner	Dog Beautician	Telephonist
Priest	Secretary	Fireman
Florist	Psychiatrist	Roadsweeper
Doctor	Writer	Weightlifter
Policeman	Gardener	Musician
Carpenter	Market Trader	Builder
Actor	Traffic Warden	Photographer
Golfer	Seamstress	TV Host
Watchmaker	Grocer	Estate Agent
Chemist	Business Man	Nanny
Undertaker	Private Detective	Club DJ

In pairs or a group, arrange for the characters to meet and develop a situation ensuing from the point of the meeting.

FACIAL EXPRESSION

Facial expression is a vital part of our non-verbal communication. Our personality is etched on our faces by permanent lines that build up such as 'laughter lines' around the eyes, or from furrows that can crease a forehead. Equally important are the transient expressions which give a visible commentary to others on what we are thinking and feeling at each moment in time. *Ray Birdwhistell estimated that the human face produces 250,000 different emotions – an astonishing total indeed.

Coupled with the use of the face as a major means of non-verbal communication is the orientation of the head, capable of many degrees of movement and angle which can make vast differences in how we use it and how we are perceived.

We read expressions in others almost subconsciously, but don't often stop to evaluate our own.

The following exercises are tailored towards helping the student identify and become aware of head use as well as to interpret reaction to different sensations.

STATES OF AWARENESS

Try this head-orientation work, for some riveting effects on the psyche.

Walk normally around the room. Stop, then continue the walk, this time leading with the head down.

How does this feel? Generally, it affords feelings of introspection.

Now walk leading with the nose out and so experience how this feels. Again, generally, it brings out feelings of inquisitiveness.

Finally, walk with the chin up, which often engenders feelings of haughtiness.

* Ray Birdwhistell (1918-1994). An American Professor of Communication whose approach to the study of kinesics was through cultural anthropology.

FACIAL PLAY

Collect or draw three cartoon pictures of facial states:

Happy   Sad   Angry

Note how the cartoonist usually exaggerates the features of the face in portraying these emotions.

Concentrate on one emotion at a time and, starting with a neutral face, practise the degrees of expression which need to be worked through before aiming at the peak of the emotion. Work for eight different stages from neutral to final facial position. Move up through each stage, consciously and deliberately, then back down again.

REACTION

Physical:

- being splashed in the face with cold water
- a bad headache
- coming out into bright sunlight
- peering in the dark

External:

- looking through a microscope
- watching a tiny insect

- smelling cabbage boiling
- smelling a beautiful flower

- hearing a strange sound
- eavesdropping on a conversation you know you shouldn't

Internal:

- Happy! It's your birthday!
- Nervous – waiting for an audition
- Sad – the holiday is over

HEAD NOTES

Different ways of using the head:

- listening sympathetically to a depressed friend
- puzzling over what to do
- watching a tense moment in the Big Match
- looking at something you can't believe is happening

Watching a tense moment in the Big Match

THE BODY

Using the body purposefully is not often a conscious effort – for the most part. Historically, our clothes today allow for a much greater freedom of movement and casual posture. Current fashions in footwear such as *Doc Martens* and loafers encourage an everyday stance and movement which is well supported by hard-wearing, practical shoes.

Let's start with a look at posture. Sit in a comfortable position on an upright chair. Now try having a conversation with another person who is:

- standing close to you
- sitting on the floor
- has their back half-turned to you
- sitting close to you, but in an upright position with their arms folded and legs crossed

See how important posture is?

Now onto some exercises for the body. This is one area where people who have had some experience in dance are at an advantage, as the need to 'pull up' from the abdomen is necessarily conscious, giving the body a sense of control and purpose.

CLOWNING AROUND

Move, so that the whole body is floppy and relaxed in the mood engendered by a clown costume.

Express states of happiness/sadness through this relaxed posture and movement.

CLOTHES HORSE

Move in ways which focus on specific parts of the body as directed by the clothes that are worn:

- stiff suit and collar
- ballgown

- swimming costume
- football/hockey/tennis kit
- tutu
- leather trousers
- pencil skirt
- leggings

HAPPY FAMILIES – a group activity:

Like the popular card game, create groups of four where each person is a member of a particular family. You can invent your own where each family creates links within itself through attributes such as personality, occupation, hobbies etc – to present a composite 'Look'.

EPISODE FROM A BOOK, PLAY OR FILM

This mime assists the application of knowledge from a written or visual source. It requires clear sequencing and the skills of character portrayal, along with attention to shape and tempo of the episode.

A group exercise such as Survival can encourage the systematic development of a scene as well as group interaction.

Survival:

The students take on the role of shipwrecked passengers and crew who are lying on a beach having been swept ashore after battling with the force of the sea and perils of a capsized ship. Gradually, they get up, dazed and tired in search of some fresh water and shade. They find someone they remember from the ship – it could be a sister, friend or perhaps one of the crew who has been hurt – and in pairs, mime their experiences. The pairs meet another pair and the mood becomes hopeful and stronger as each group resolves to form a shelter and look after each other. Engrossed in their work, the survivors do not hear or see that they are being watched. Slowly, there is a growing awareness of the intruders surrounding them and the mood becomes fearful. Groups of four join other groups until there is one protective huddle against the intruders. One person is chosen to go forward and meet the strangers, which he does tentatively, arms raised in submission. The rest of the group watch in tense concentration, until the spokesman smiles in relief at the sustenance offered by the strangers and the tension breaks. The group form a support line to pass the food and drink to a central spot and, having thanked their helpers, sit down to enjoy their repast.

CONTACT WITH AN IMAGINARY PERSON AND OBJECT

Contact with anyone or anything imaginary is technically demanding in terms of accuracy and attention to detail if the communication is to be believable. This depends greatly on the precision of the actions and reactions of the performer and thus exercises in observation and concentration are valuable.

Working with real people and objects, prior to the medium of imaginary contact, is a sound start.

PEOPLE CONTACT

Observation – altered appearance

Face each other in pairs.

Take a good look at each other's appearance. Turn your backs on one another and change three things about your appearance. Face each other again and try to identify the alterations made.

Concentration – Mirror Mirror

In pairs, tune into this exercise by taking it in turns to mirror each other's movements – slowly!

Extending from this, one person gets ready to go out whilst the partner acts as the mirror. Try the following as a person and the reflection:

- brushing your hair and arranging it into a particular style. Be adventurous!
- putting on a hat for a wedding/football match/river walk
- putting on a balaclava

- wrapping a scarf around your neck
- putting on a fancy dress mask

Mirror Scenes

A mirror scene is one in which two people enact a scenario in front of a mirror whilst two others are the reflections. Try the following, creating a short scene of action as:

- a beautician and customer
- a dance teacher and student
- a film star and make up artist
- a sales assistant and customer
- two members of a pop band getting ready for a concert

Mirror Scenes – a dance teacher and student

Mimes demonstrating contact with imaginary people

These can be performed individually or as a duologue. If two people are to work together, make sure that the performers create different reactions to the imaginary person in order to maintain variety within the mime:

- teaching someone to dance
- measuring a customer for a suit
- taking orders in a restaurant
- having a manicure
- working as a magician's assistant
- giving a haircut

Invent a personality and physical type for your imaginary person – be as varied as you like.

OBJECT CONTACT

Observation – Balloons

Develop the awareness of contrast between the real and the imagined. Blow up a balloon and feel the change in shape and texture as you do so. Now the fiddly bit at the end – how do *you* tie up a balloon?

Repeat the exercise, this time working from memory. Try to recall the physical changes that occurred as you blew up the balloon. See how accurate you can be in tying up the balloon.

– Sludge

In a group, pass round a ball of imaginary 'sludge', a pretend ball of malleable material, from which you mould an everyday object. Now use it for people to guess what it is. How accurate were you in showing the object?

Concentration – House of Cards

Imagine you have a pack of cards and you are building a card house. Concentrate on placing each card at a time without letting the card house fall.

– Tile Decoration

Have an imaginary tile in front of you and decorate it in some way. This could be by free hand painting, stencilled patterns, charcoal and chalks etc. Try to visualise the texture of the tile, colour of the design, thickness of the brush, chalks and so on.

HAND CONTROL

Exercises for hand control are beneficial at this level because the technical demands of sustaining credible contact with an imaginary object are high.

The following exercise concentrates initially on developing the dexterity of hand movement and then puts it into practice to achieve greater precision and accuracy in the representation of objects.

1. Hold both hands out flat with palms down. Proceed with the following using both hands simultaneously:

- isolate the thumb by opening it at right angles to the fingers. Return to a closed hand position

- isolate the thumb and index finger from the rest of the hand and then close

- repeat for the middle finger, index and thumb

- isolate the little finger from the rest of the hand and return

2. Hold both hands out flat and in front of you again. This time, you are going to pick up objects of varying sizes using only the relevant parts of the hand to do so:

- start with a small glass bead. Pick up the bead using the thumb and index finger of either your left or right hand

- hold the imaginary bead, consciously keeping the remaining fingers apart. Try to keep the fingers not in use, straight and together. This enhances the clarity of the action and prevents it from being muffled by imprecise hand gesture

- transfer the bead to the thumb and index finger of your opposite hand, then release the finger and thumb that was originally holding the bead. (See Fig 3)

Fig 3

- repeat the transfer several times, working for clean, uncluttered movement

Apply the same procedure to different configurations of the fingers and thumb, making the object bigger each time you add another finger!

Thus, examples of picking items up with thumb/index finger might be:

glass bead   **paper clip**   **rail ticket**

With thumb/index/middle finger:

purse   **book**   **hairbrush**

With thumb/index/middle/fourth finger:

mobile phone   **roll of paper**

Whole hand:

ball   **bag of crisps**   **sponge**

Remember to try the same exercise in different spatial orientations. For example:

from the side:

tin can   **cup**   **glass bottle**

from underneath:

holding onto a tube rail   **fixing a ceiling tile**

Mimes demonstrating contact with imaginary objects

Scrambled Eggs:

This is an exercise in which you *are* the object. Physically thinking yourself into the object will increase your awareness of size, shape and consistency and be of help when you come to mime contact with imaginary objects.

Work from concrete items where you have a very visual frame of reference, to abstract concepts which require more from you in terms of drawing on imaginative recall.

The activities can be worked upon by individuals, pairs or groups. Items represented by a group can be great fun – for example, try a washing machine in which each person is an integral component.

Concrete items might be:

toaster	ice cream	fire	parachute
sponge	book	television	polo mint

Scrambled Eggs – fire

Abstract ideas might be:

a windy night	a stampede
an evening reception	children's games
a hot beach	a dark road

MIMES

Contact with these imaginary objects can be performed individually or in pairs. If two players are involved, maintain the contrast of reactions given by each performer to enhance the spontaneity:

- pumping up a bicycle tyre
- painting a mural
- icing a cake
- cleaning windows
- emptying a safe
- decorating a Christmas tree
- manoeuvering a boat
- stuffing a turkey
- washing the car

SUMMARY

It is hoped that the information and activities in this handbook have provided a starting point for ways in which you might develop the subject further.

The first four grades of the LAMDA mime syllabus offer students the scope to develop a high level of proficiency in terms of the fusion of artistic merit and technical ability.

This is all important to Grades V, VI and the Mime Medal of the syllabus, which require a degree of speciality from the candidate (for example, the mime of a character from the Commedia dell' Arte). These are exciting and challenging areas of mime, into which it is hoped that enterprising students will venture, having first of all secured a firm foundation from which to develop.

SUGGESTED READING

Awareness Through Movement – M Feldenkreis

Body Watching – D Morris

Drama Starters – G Stoate

Exploring Mime – M Stolzenberg

Gamesters' Handbook – D Brandes and H Phillips

100+ Ideas for Drama – A Scher and C Verrall

Laban for Actors and Dancers – J Newlove

The Actor and His Body – L Pisk

The Alexander Principle – W Barlow

Theatre Games for Young Performers – M Novelly

Theatre Movement: The Actor and His Space – N King

Patricia Hammond

IMPROVISATION

INTRODUCTION

The lunatic, the lover and the poet
are of imagination all compact.

William Shakespeare

Imagination is a wonderful gift! It is the seed from which all truly creative work springs.

If we are to help our students realise their full creative potential we need to provide imaginative stimuli in order to eliminate mechanical responses.

Improvisation can be very helpful here and, if structured imaginatively, can help our students to achieve conviction, intensity, confidence, dramatic awareness and spontaneity within their interpretation or performance.

The various elements essential for vital and spontaneous performance may all be stimulated, encouraged and developed through improvisation. The imaginative process is one of constant learning and change. We must always be adaptable, flexible and sensitive both to the needs of our individual students and to the performance itself.

This handbook is intended as a guide to teachers who may be preparing students for LAMDA examinations. Although the examinations may take the form of Group, Duologue or Solo entries, many exercises are suggested which are intended for the class as a whole, as I believe it is of great value to involve all students for the greater part of any session wherever possible. This aids communication and group awareness, encourages the exchange of ideas and inter-action, and also promotes confidence throughout the whole group. This approach also alleviates any boredom which may ensue if too much time is spent on individual work when teaching larger classes. Solo and duologue ideas can grow from this initial group exploration, and exercises are suggested for this development.

The benefits of improvisation cannot be underestimated – very exciting results can be achieved and a more intensified performance may be realised.

Through improvisation we can stimulate or develop the following:

- imagination
- dramatic awareness
- group awareness
- self confidence
- clarity
- communication
- sensitivity
- sincerity
- reaction and inter-action
- dramatic shape
- fluency
- spontaneity
- conviction
- vitality
- intensity

Teachers may well find that the Improvisation examinations will be of real value when used in conjunction with other subjects within the LAMDA syllabus. Many of the ideas suggested here may work equally well in helping students to prepare for The Speaking of Verse and Prose, Mime, Choral Speaking and Acting examinations.

I have used many of the ideas and exercises with my own students with success, although surprises will always be in store. Be prepared to be flexible and to grow with your students – their fund of ideas will be inexhaustible if you merely unlock the door to their imagination...

RELAXATION

Any teacher will know that physical tension and inhibition need to be overcome in order to release students both mentally and physically.

Music can be very helpful here.

GROUP EXERCISE 1

With suitable music let your students find a comfortable position to lie down on their own ideal island. This is a time for quiet contemplation and the sole purpose here is to encourage mental relaxation. On this island anything is possible and students could be asked to think about their ideal surroundings, climate and location. Ask them also to reflect "What would they most like to achieve?" "Who would they most like to be?", "Who would be their ideal companions?" etc.

Total relaxation should be encouraged – questions should be asked softly and music chosen to enhance this atmosphere.

There are many titles within the syllabus which could be used effectively for the purpose of relaxation. Many are broad-based and are open to diverse interpretation. Take for instance a subject such as "A Parcel" or "A Mysterious Box" – titles such as these may easily be used for imaginative relaxation.

GROUP EXERCISE 2

With each student working in his or her own space, let each create their own parcel or box. Music again may be used here to suggest atmosphere. Each student can lift the box well above the head (stretching) and drop it again (relaxing). Encourage movement in all directions, pushing it to the sides and passing it behind, pushing it away from the body diagonally, lifting it with the feet, balancing it on the head and so on. Each student will find their own ways of moving their own parcel individually. It is important to encourage stretching and relaxing. The students should sit in a relaxed and comfortable position at the conclusion.

GROUP EXERCISE 3

Still using the idea of an imaginary parcel, students can form a circle and pass the parcel, opening it only when the music stops to show what is inside. This can be arranged with several parcels moving simultaneously, all of different weights and sizes.

Suggestions from students were as follows: a snake, a helium balloon, a kitten, an umbrella, a jack-in-the-box and a severed hand! This idea could be further developed by arranging the group in pairs with each linking their two objects in a short scene.

GROUP EXERCISE 4

Again with the use of music, preferably humorous, all students become an item of washing, e.g. socks, trousers, pyjamas, towels etc. They all enter the washing machine, tightly packed, and the cycle begins. This can cause great mirth, but laughter is one of the valuable releases for tension – the music will control the action if cleverly chosen and entangled clothes may move, swirl and jostle in the water. The spinning action creates opportunity for energetic movement, as everyone swirls closely together curling very tightly. Physical contact should be encouraged here. The machine finally stops and everyone is still in a totally relaxed position. Students can then create lines of washing on a windy day and can "blow" in the wind with maximum stretching movements. Finally the washing is comfortably arranged (relaxed position). This could be further developed maybe with conversations between the inanimate items.

Choral speaking could be a further development with 6 or 8 speakers vocally creating the noises of the machine. The use of word dynamics such as "Sh Sh Sh Sh Shhhhhhh" "Whirr Whirrr Whirrrrrrr!" "Woo-eee Woo-eee Woo-eeeeeee" "Spinnnnnnn – Spinnnnnn" etc. could be used. There should be no lack of ideas. This exercise not only aids relaxation but stimulates imagination and encourages physical contact. It can work equally well with any machine, with suitable adaptation. My students developed this idea when working on the elemental theme of "Water".

Relaxation is essential to ensure imaginative and creative responses. Exercises such as these encourage mental and physical relaxation, help to relieve tension and to increase physical freedom. Students learn to inter-act both physically and mentally without embarrassment or inhibition.

NATURALNESS AND SPONTANEITY

So often we tell our students that their work is mechanical and contrived or lacks spontaneity – here are some ideas which may be useful in achieving natural responses and a convincing performance.

GROUP EXERCISE 1

In a large circle take a line with a broad meaning which could have many interpretations, for example: "Why on earth did you do that?"

The first student says this to any other student in the circle who must reply instantly, for example: "Well I couldn't help it – there was a chimpanzee on my shoulder!" The second student should then repeat the line to any other student, maybe with a different tone or implication "Why on earth did you do that?" Again an immediate response must be given, for example: "I thought it was a good idea at the time." and so on until everyone has participated.

This can be further developed by duologue work with each pair continuing a short conversation.

Other useful lines for this exercise may be:

- If only you'd told me before.
- OH! It's you!
- I don't know how to tell you this.
- This WOULD happen tonight!
- I am not going to ask you again!

And for more action and movement the following may be effective:

- Quick hide!
- Help me to push it!

- It's right up there – oh no!

- Can't you keep still for one minute?

Exercises such as these are also very useful in helping students to think "on their feet" and can be immensely valuable when training students to tackle spontaneous improvisation which is demanded with the improvisation syllabus.

GROUP EXERCISE 2

A simple situation may be given e.g. a person is threatening to jump from a tall building.

The group, one by one or in twos or threes, join the crowd with immediate responses to the situation.

Here are the reactions of one group:

a: Oh look! Look up there! He's going to jump!

b: Look Mavis – he's going to jump – fetch the police!

c: Where's the 'phone?

d: I'll go – oh no – he's getting nearer the edge!

All: Don't jump! Don't do it!

d: What's happening – Oh no – it's my husband!

e: Calm down – someone's gone for the police.

f: Your husband you say? What have you done to make him do this? If I were him I would jump! Jump go on! She's not worth it!

All: No! *No! Don't jump!*

The advantage with exercises like this is that everyone has a central focus of attention and group involvement releases inhibitions.

This could become the basis for duologue work as each pair of characters discusses the crisis and reveals their involvement with the victim.

GROUP EXERCISE 3

Again, immediate response is demanded but this time it is concerned more with movement, physical contact, group awareness and inter-action. By using various locations (e.g. a Church) students are simply given a number 1, 2, 3 etc. according to the number of members in the group. If for instance he were given "A Church" No 1 starts the scene. He may decide that he is the bridegroom waiting at the altar and without any discussion No 2 joins the action, maybe as a bride or a vicar. No 3 may join as a bellringer and so on until the scene is complete. Initially, Mime is preferable until your group is secure, then speech may be introduced.

Once a scene has been explored the exercise may be repeated with a new location, and a new numbering sequence of students will ensure that everyone has a chance to become a "leader".

Other locations may be as follows:

- a supermarket
- a library
- an eastern market
- a playground
- a fairground
- an airport lounge
- a doctor's waiting room
- a hairdressing salon
- a café or theatre bar

GROUP EXERCISE 4

This exercise is popular particularly with younger pupils and again ensures spontaneous response.

Two class members should be chosen to play the Shopkeeper and the Customer, the remainder play the items in the shop.

The Customer, playing a character of his or her choice, converses with the Shopkeeper (again in chosen character) and asks to see some particular item, for example:

- fruit
- clowns
- animals
- sporting personalities
- rare pre-historic monsters
- computers

It could be whatever the Customer chooses and I have known younger members to ask to see bars of chocolates, sweets, a ball of string, a ballet dancer and the Loch Ness Monster! The class immediately takes up a frozen position of the item requested and the Shopkeeper describes each one briefly according to how he or she sees it, as the Customer is taken on tour of the shop. The Customer makes a selection and pays for the selected "item". Fictitious (and sometimes unrealistic) prices can be charged by the Shopkeeper to add to the fun. The selected person becomes the new Shopkeeper and the original Shopkeeper then plays the Customer and so on.

This exercise is especially valuable when a class requires discipline and concentration – any movement or unnecessary noise leads to disqualification!

Sounds or verbal responses may be introduced at a later stage e.g. talking dolls, animated toys, musical boxes, computers etc. The ideas of your students will hopefully astound you!

This exercise can be developed by working in pairs according to character or object – many interesting conversations will take place between two inanimate objects – this all serves to stimulate the imagination.

GROUP EXERCISE 5

In order to heighten awareness of the senses and therefore increase conviction and spontaneity within an improvised scene, the following exercises may be useful.

SIGHT

The group moves around in pairs. One is blindfolded, the other acts as a guide: then roles are reversed. This increases trust and, by removing the sense of sight, greater awareness is gained. The "seeing" partner needs also to increase observation in order to impart visual information to the blindfolded partner.

SOUND

In pairs, let one student silently mouth a simple message, completely unvoiced. Only by lip reading may the partner gauge the meaning. To develop this further the pairs may work on a short scene using mime and gesture to gain emphasis. As usual, reverse the roles so that all students can experience the lack of hearing.

TOUCH

With simple improvised text each student must touch his or her partner with every line. For example:

a: Hello George. I haven't seen you in months. (*Handshake.*)

b: Hello Sally. (*Continues handshake.*)

a: Well, you do look smart. (*Pats his jacket with admiration.*) What's the occasion?

b: (*Taking her to one side.*) I can't talk now.

a: (*Patting his head.*) George, are you feeling alright? – you seem very hot.

b: (*Grabbing her arm.*) Well no, actually I'm... I'm...

Students could be invited to finish scenes such as this but with particular attention to meaningful physical contact. So often a lack of physical contact and expression can result in a mechanical and unnatural performance. Like so many exercises, these can sometimes produce some hilarious reactions but sometimes intensely dramatic performances can result.

Awareness of all the senses is extremely important – a lack of awareness can cause students to isolate themselves from their fellow actors.

To encourage physical freedom within exercises such as this will relieve tension and build up physical confidence. Performances will be more convincing if this is achieved.

EMOTIONAL BREATHING

I have often noticed that so much conviction and spontaneity within interpretation relies heavily upon breathing.

We are all aware of the need for relaxation, breath control and resonance to fully release the voice but so often emotional breathing is overlooked in performance. I call it emotional breathing because it springs entirely from the actor's emotional state of mind.

Consider the natural mechanism of breathing for the following:

- a sigh of relief
- a gasp of delight

Always the natural verbal or audible reaction is preceded by a reactionary breath.

We can consider other possibilities – the clues lie in our everyday language.

- to catch your breath – *a sudden gasp to support a simple shock*
- to hold your breath – *at times of tension or excitement*
- to take a deep breath – *in a situation of difficulty, again to support the difficulty or adversity ahead*
- to take your breath away – *an expression of absolute delight*
- to breathe a sigh of relief – *an expulsion of air when support is no longer required*
- to save your breath – *a situation which is not even worth speaking about. Often conveyed with a frustrated sigh*
- to take a breather – *to relax*
- to breathe a sigh of relief – *accentuated excitement*
- heavy breathing
- to breathe your last

Much attention is given to breathing with regard to the vocal mechanism in order to release the voice and control the breathing, but without *imaginative* attention to breathing the reaction will never be spontaneous.

Breathing is fundamental to the actor. At birth we take our first breath and upon our exit from the world we "breathe our last". Awareness of the need for imaginative or emotional breathing will not only intensify the performance but will be vocally more convincing. The voice will respond according to the mood or situation. So often we ask our students to laugh or to cry or to convey varying degrees of these extremes. When analysed, the crying or sobbing process is an erratic intake of breath – the more erratic and quick in pace, the more intense.

Laughter conversely is a release of breath – Hahh – Hahh – Hahhhh. This is a simple fact but often overlooked. Therefore, within a scene where laughter or tears have been significant,the actor will need to gradually recover his normal breathing patterns before he or she can speak with utter control. So often great attention is given to the crying action but all conviction and spontaneity is lost because an actor immediately resumes a normal tone to continue with the dialogue when in fact the breathing would take time to recover and would not allow this to happen.

There are varying degrees of laughter and tears, and all can be explored within your class through the breathing process:

- holding back tears
- crying softly
- sobbing
- screaming hysterically
- a silent scream (*extreme fear or emotion*)
- a smile
- polite laughter
- a giggle
- holding back a fit of the giggles

- hearty laughter
- hysterical or uncontrolled laughter

Imaginative and appropriate situations can be found with ease if these are to be explored in class.

The breathing becomes, or should become, more pronounced as the list progresses. The state of mind regulates our breathing process and this should be actively encouraged within performance. It is, for example, the act of trying to withhold breath to control the giggles, the insistent breath tries to escape and, with mouth closed, the result is a series of ridiculous grimaces and, in extreme cases, protuberant eyes and puffed cheeks.

Audible screams require extreme breath support – they stem from a gasp of shock and the extreme tension of the vocal mechanism results in a high pitched scream. The silent scream is of course a result of ultimate vocal tension.

Having explored the influence of emotional breath we can introduce another simple exercise to develop this awareness.

Within any dialogue, reaction is essential. Let each pair work as follows:

a: speaks the lines of text of improvised speech

b: reacts solely with breath

Then reverse the process giving each student a chance to explore the breathing reactions. This will make your student more aware of the need for emotional breathing whilst listening, and it will greatly intensify the reaction. It will also help to ensure that the vocal tone and facial reactions are plausible in response.

For example:

a: I don't know how to tell you this.

b: (*Takes breath.*)

a: (*Breathing for support.*) It isn't easy. (*Breathes again.*) It's about your sister.

b: (*Breathing urgently.*) Why, what's happened?

a: (*Breathing more erratically.*) She's... she's...

b: (*Breathing in panic.*) What... please tell me.

a: She's – she's not your sister.

b: (*Gasp of shock – pause.*)

Over-reaction may be the initial result but once your students have mastered this art and explored it imaginatively you will notice how this will bring subtlety, conviction and sensitivity to their performance.

CHARACTER

The creation of a character is an exciting and on-going process. No character should be static but it should develop through situation and circumstance. In order to avoid stereo-typed characterization it is a useful idea to give your students a questionnaire to help them think about their character in much greater depth.

This fund of information will be useful in the development of ideas and will arm the inhibited actor with facts about his character leading therefore to a more secure performance.

QUESTIONNAIRE

- name of character
- age
- address
- nationality
- occupation if any
- number of brothers and sisters
- type of accommodation lived in
- favourite food
- favourite colour
- Do you keep a pet – if so, which?
- Where do you like to go on holiday?
- Which (if any) television programme do you like to watch?
- Name your favourite hobbies and interests
- What annoys you most?
- Describe your two greatest friends
- Are you rich/poor/in between?
- Where did you (do you) go to school?
- Are you religious – if so which religion?

Describe briefly the following:

- your most frightening experience
- when you last lost your temper
- your most exciting experience
- your favourite clothes
- your most upsetting experience
- the person you most admire and why
- where or how you spent your last holiday
- your favourite author/poet/film
- your favourite season
- your chief qualities and faults
- what makes you laugh – describe a funny experience
- what you were doing yesterday, last month, last year
- what you may be doing tomorrow

Please add any other details which may be appropriate and draw a sketch or cartoon showing your major physical characteristics.

Please also bring one stage prop to the next session which may be appropriate for your particular character e.g. wand, duster, cardboard box.

In my own class we created, through this process, a fascinating assortment of characters as follows:

a. a devoted Irish nun who was sympathetic but totally impractical aged 37

b. a Scots nurse with many frustrations about her difficult family

c. a bungling yet eager old Etonian news reporter aged 22

d. a lazy, bored American unemployed father who watched his goldfish all day

e. a cardboard city alcoholic

f. Lady Camilla-Jayne Davenport-Smythe aged 29½

g: a chic Parisian poodle-owning model who shop-lifted for amusement

h: a deferential and forgetful vicar who fished by the river to escape his bossy and over-powering wife

i: a disabled ex-businessman who now worked as a petrol forecourt attendant

These characters, when paired, produced some extremely interesting duologues and could cope quite readily with spontaneous work. Various titles, situations and themes created opportunity to further explore the characters. Because of the security of the characterization students were able to respond spontaneously with very little discussion or preparation. Reactions were sharp, responses were immediate and the improvisation gained dramatic intensity as a result of the sound character analysis.

EMOTIONAL RESPONSES

The exploration of emotional responses can heighten our student's awareness and thereby add sincerity and conviction to his performance.

Contrasting responses to a particular emotion can further extend our student's sensitivity. Reflection upon this aspect can help to eliminate a mechanical or stereo-typed reaction within the actor and encourage imaginative and flexible thinking. If worked in conjunction with characterization the results can be very evocative.

As always, I would involve the whole class or group at the outset to allow everyone to explore the various emotions. Here are some suggestions, although I know that experienced teachers will readily find appropriate situations to stimulate imagination.

FEAR

- Terrorists have entered the room – no one must move

GUILT

- Your birthday party has ended in disaster – a fire has caused the death of several guests – you face the relatives of the victims
- You have been caught in the act of shop-lifting

HAPPINESS

- A benevolent headmistress/boss has announced an unexpected two week holiday
- You are hostages and are told by your captors that you are now free

DESPAIR

- You are all trapped underground. You are weak and have no hope of being discovered

ENVY

- Your rival group has won a month's trip to some exotic island

- Your audition has been a disaster but your rich good-looking friend has been chosen for the leading role

For practical purposes the group can explore the emotion silently but in order to develop this further, two or three students could volunteer to lead the speech, allowing the remainder of the group to react accordingly to the situation.

Smaller groups could then move to explore contrasting responses to the same emotion. A small group of my students worked on the theme of *grief* with the following result.

MOTHER (*Played by Sarah aged 16*)

She was the best daughter anybody could ever have asked for. (*Pause.*) I mean, she had everything going for her: her looks, her personality, her job ... and then this happened ... and I would just like to know why, why her? Why my daughter when there are so many bad people in this wicked world? If there is a God then he moves in mysterious ways. I just want her back, I miss her so much. (*Breaks down in tears.*)

JEALOUS FRIEND (*Played by Laura aged 16*)

Well, if you ask me she deserved all she got. I tried to tell her, I really did, but ... she knew best. She always went with the wrong men. It was hopeless. Well ... maybe she's learned her lesson now?

TRUE FRIEND (*Played by Annabel aged 17*)

How could this have happened to her? How could she leave me like this – all alone – I can't cope without her. I can't go on – who could have killed her?

ANOTHER FRIEND (*Played by Chloe aged 14*)

Who could have hated her enough to destroy her? She was a wonderful person – kind and in the prime of life. Who could have done it?

A BOYFRIEND (*Played by Daniel aged 17*)

Everyone thought I loved her – everyone only saw the good side of her – but I knew her – really knew her – and knowing her wasn't easy. I did it ... yes, I killed her.

These are just some examples of contrasting responses to an emotion. Here we see genuine reactions to grief and also self-pity, triumph and self-justification. Group exercises such as this can lead to interesting work, either solo or duologue. Exploration of any emotion such as this can lead to deeper understanding and intensity in performance.

THE SYLLABUS

The syllabus is structured with six progressive grades plus a final examination and covers a wide range of creative stimuli. The titles are broad-based to allow maximum creative expression. Your students will find an inexhaustible fund of ideas.

One word alone, for example, *party* can be the key to many devised and spontaneous pieces.

For example, the birthday party, a surprise party, a forbidden party, a political party, a party-political broadcast, a picnic, a noisy party, a disastrous party, a party dress, a fancy dress party.

Or, if the theme were *numbers:*

> A house number, a telephone number, a dress size number, a passport number, a prisoner's number, a number of guests or tickets, a theatre ticket number, a bus number, a flight number, a train number, a raffle ticket

These are but a few suggestions, and experienced teachers will readily find alternatives. The important point is to encourage imaginative and original approaches to a given subject or title.

Shakespearean, Commedia dell' Arte or fictitious characters can be explored with great success through improvisation. With boldness and imagination we could find Titania and Bottom in a modern day launderette, or Petruchio and Kate at a health farm. Perhaps Romeo and Juliet meet in heaven in the after-life, or Mr Toad attends an advanced motorist's course, or maybe Jean Brodie may visit Portobello Road – anything is possible!

The Elements provide excellent stimulation for improvisation. The use of music, poetry, mime, speech, choral speech, movement and dance can all be linked together in diverse ways to explore various themes.

Here are some suggestions for various interpretations:

FIRE

The Great Fire of London, bush fires, passion, firing squads, bonfires, Guy Fawkes, smoking, terrorists, coal fires, firemen, bomb attacks, accidents, birthday candles

EARTH

Environmental issues, the seasons, outer-space travellers, from seed to harvest, animals, trees, gardens, underground, mines, caves, pot-holing, earthquakes

AIR

Pollution, winds, gales and hurricanes, air travel, space travel, suffocation, balloons, whirlwinds, birds, airborne germs, radio waves

WATER

Drought, an oasis, the oceans, shipwreck, water-divining, cruise liners, fishing boats, seaside, goldfish, garden ponds, sewers, rivers and waterfalls, moats, sailing, rain, monsoon, umbrellas, bridges, deep sea diving, snow and ice

Below is an example of a short group improvisation worked out by my students over a two day period. They were each asked to write some brief lines about *ice* – it is not possible to print them all but here are several:

CHLOE (*Aged 14 years*)

With much huffing of breath and rubbing of hands, I managed to clear a small space on my window, and on peering through ... what wonder I saw! Everything was dressed in white. The snow was falling, swirling and whirling, obscuring my view.

FIONA (*Aged 11 years*)

A crack spreads like a bolt of lightning in the sky,
Beneath, freezing waters paralyse lifeless fish.
Glistening in the early February dawn
The sparkling ice disintegrates.

HOLLY (*Aged 11 years*)

Nuts, strawberries and cream,
Vanilla and chocolate ice cream,
Coffee, pistachio, lemon ice,
Every one of those is nice.

SARAH (*Aged 16 years*)

Slippery as glass
Cold as stone,
Sparkling like champagne,
Glistening like rain.

These lines and those of the rest of the group were linked together to form an abstract dance drama. With the use of suitable atmospheric music the group presented *Ice* starting with a child's viewpoint and finishing more philosophically with old age – *The Winter of Life.* It was interesting here to note that mixed age groups worked effectively together.

The syllabus offers through improvisation, many exciting and creative opportunities for dramatic interpretation to students of all levels and all ages. Imagination is the key to all true creative expression and I leave you with the words of William Shakespeare:

> *The best in this kind are but shadows; and the*
> *worse are no worse, if imagination amend them.*

Theseus, A Midsummer Night's Dream, Act 5 Sc i